HOW TO DRAW INSECTS

HOW TO DRAW
INSECTS

by

NORMAN WEAVER, FSIA

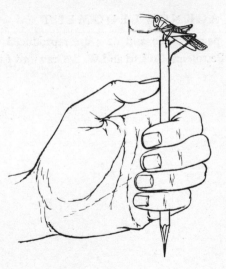

THE STUDIO PUBLICATIONS

LONDON & NEW YORK

ACKNOWLEDGMENT

The drawings on pages 58, 60 and 62-4 are reproduced by courtesy
of Shell Petroleum Co Ltd and W. S. Crawford Ltd

Published in London by The Studio Limited, Hulton House, Fleet Street, EC4
and in New York by The Studio Publications Inc, 432 *Fourth Avenue:*
printed in England by Bradford and Dickens, Drayton House, London, WC1

CONTENTS

INTRODUCTION

FOR many people, insects hold but very little interest. They are small creatures, somewhat creepy, and must be crushed or swatted on sight. There are, of course, many whose habits bring them into the category of pests, that must in the interests of human welfare be destroyed. By and large though, they deserve our greatest respect. Regarded as pieces of mechanical design, they approach perfection, and are probably the most efficient life-form on earth. They must also be the most versatile, for they are possessed of immense strength for their weight, they can leap relatively enormous heights and distances, run at fantastic speeds,

above: Brush sketch of a cicada, a Methuselah of the insect world, said to spend seventeen years of its life underground.

swim or walk on water, fly, hover, burrow, and walk upside down. They can adapt themselves for survival under almost any terrestial condition from the Equator to the Poles. Some species exist in brine, others in hot springs; one even spends its early life in petroleum puddles in the oil fields of South America. They are masters of disguise, mimicry and camouflage, efficient engineers, craftsmen, chemists and farmers. In beauty of colour and form they can equal the most exotic flower or bird. The horn-like substance (chitin) of which they are chiefly composed, is tough, resilient, waterproof; acid, alkali and rot resistant and, save by actual crushing, almost indestructible. The existence of any one group would be miracle enough, yet their myriad species far outnumber those of all other terrestial animals combined; and many were in existence millions of years ago, long before the appearance of man.

Although I have had to use entomological terms in the text, this book is concerned only with ways and means of drawing insects, it is not a book on entomology. I would like to take the opportunity that this introduction affords, of stating that such knowledge that I have of the science of entomology, I have gleaned by flagrantly picking the brains of various experts in this field, who have always submitted most cheerfully to the process. Since I shall have to continue to rely upon this source of information for future work, it is imperative that I keep them friendly, hence this admission. The real object of this book is to introduce you to, and interest you in, a subject for drawing that offers endless variety, in the hope that you will find it in every way as absorbing as I do myself.

*   *   *   *   *

Readers in any part of the world with no local or available naturalists' supplier, may be interested in the address of the people with whom I deal. They are:

Watkins & Doncaster, 110 Parkview Road, Welling, Kent, England, who can supply you with any of the materials recommended in the text, either by post or by personal call. No doubt there are similar specialists in most other countries: an enquiry at a natural history museum would doubtless provide the information.

EQUIPMENT

WHEN I had to tackle my first insect drawings, what I lacked in experience I more than made up for in enthusiasm. I had the fixed idea that for this sort of work, an expensive microscope was a must. I promptly, far too promptly, bought myself a handsome compound instrument that I could ill afford. I am still immensely proud of the thing, and would not be without it, but for the work for which it was originally bought, it was quite unsuitable. Both the eyepieces and the objectives with which I had it fitted were far and away too powerful, and useless for my purpose at the time. These days, the major part of any insect work I do is drawn with the aid of simple lenses, and only low power objectives in the microscope.

My advice to anyone interested in trying his or her hand at this sort of work for the first time, is: don't imagine that an expensive instrument is essential. It isn't. Darwin did a great deal of valuable research with the aid of simple lenses. A microscope is a lovely thing to possess, but unless you intend to take up histology, do not equip it with powerful accessories. The three objectives I now use, in order of usefulness are a 3 inch × 1.7, a $1\frac{1}{2}$ inches × 3.5, and occasionally a $\frac{2}{3}$ inch × 10.

I would suggest, then, by way of basic equipment, not a microscope, but a set of good quality adjustable stand lenses, of three different powers. It is important that they be of good quality, for cheap magnifying glasses will distort, and your work will not be true.

You will also need an adjustable examination stage to hold your specimen at the desired angle for drawing. This can be either bought or made. The handyman will find no difficulty in constructing one like the right-hand illustration opposite. A disc of $\frac{3}{8}$ inch balsa wood is pivoted by a centre nut to a washer soldered to the horizontal brass rod. A small brass block is drilled and tapped in two directions, and a vertical brass rod fitted in a heavy base. Once your insect is pinned to this, it can be adjusted for height, angle and tilt without again touching the specimen. The not-so-handyman can achieve similar results, with almost as universal a

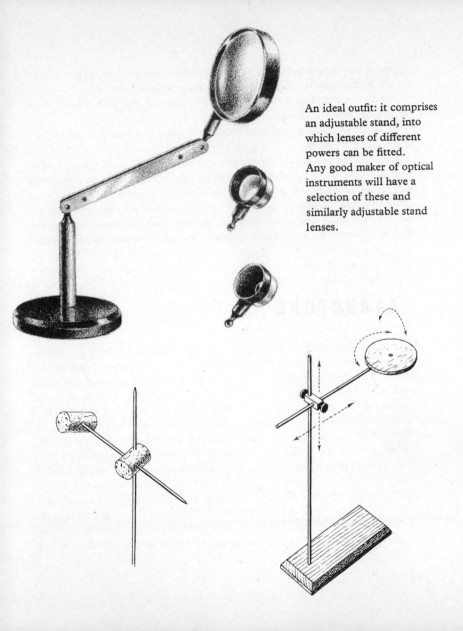

An ideal outfit: it comprises
an adjustable stand, into
which lenses of different
powers can be fitted.
Any good maker of optical
instruments will have a
selection of these and
similarly adjustable stand
lenses.

movement, by using a bill-spike, two corks and a knitting-needle, as in the other sketch. In this latter case, additional weight must be fixed to the base.

It is also essential that the work table be a robust one, otherwise either of these stages may vibrate in a maddening fashion.

In the preparation of your specimen for drawing you may also require any of the following items:

Two pairs of entomologists forceps, one pair with curved square tips and a pair with fine tips. Two or three ordinary sewing needles of different sizes mounted into wooden handles (old pen holders will serve this purpose admirably). Some insect repairing cement, to cope with any disaster immediately: two sorts are obtainable, one for bodies, antennæ etc, and the other for wings. Some pieces of $\frac{3}{8}$ and $\frac{1}{4}$ inch balsa wood and a supply of fine-gauge pins of various lengths.

STRUCTURE

THE body of an insect is made up of three main masses: the head, the thorax, and the abdomen. Although the function of these three parts is separate and distinct, visually the division is not always easy to determine, sometimes being quite misleading. The head and thorax can be joined so tightly as to appear as one, as can the thorax and the abdomen. Among the beetles one finds that a ventral section of the thorax can be extended over the lower abdomen, giving the illusion of abdominal legs, which cannot happen. In some of the 'waisted' insects, the 'waist' would appear to be the obvious division between thorax and abdomen, when in fact it really occurs between two abdominal segments, one of which is built into the thorax. A frequently recurring system throughout insect structure is very much like the row of flower-pots opposite. The pots may be flat, elongated, squat, or lopsided, but the nesting of the narrow end of one segment into the wider end of its neighbour is to be found in many of the parts, such as antennæ, tarsi, palps and cerci. Even the thorax and abdomen can sometimes have this

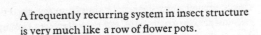

A frequently recurring system in insect structure
is very much like a row of flower pots.

appearance. Underneath its plating system, the insect is contained in an un-
broken membraneous sac, and the plates, or sclerites, are attached to this; but
we are concerned only with the exterior, and much of what we will have to draw
will be variations of our row of flower-pots.

The external anatomy of an insect, when compared with that of man, is in one
respect much easier to cope with. The insect carries its 'bone' structure, (called
the exoskeleton), on the outside, and the shapes of its component parts are not
subject to change through muscular action. Thus, for our sort of work, no knowledge of the muscular system is necessary. This advantage is offset by the fact
that, whereas in human anatomy one has useful rules of comparative proportion
as a guide to accurate drawing, no such rules are applicable to insect anatomy.
The relative proportions of parts, and parts of parts, are modified according to
the requirements of the one particular species in question. One of the principle
difficulties to be faced when drawing insects is that of seeing what precisely is
going on, either because of the smallness of the specimen, or because of obscuring
fuzz or hairs. Once the basic external anatomy is understood however, the chances
of correct interpretation are more likely.

THE HEAD

THE head is the centre of the senses. It may be provided with any of the following equipment:

Two multi-lensed, or compound, eyes, which can be enormous as in the dragonfly on page 17 or streamlined out of recognition as in the weevil, page 60, or absent altogether as with the termite soldier on page 64:

One to several single-lensed, or simple, eyes, called the ocelli; the number mostly encountered is two or three, but they are often lacking entirely.

A pair of antennæ, which grow from the epicranium near the compound eyes; these can be minute or much longer than their owner.

Three pairs of mouth parts, comprising one set of mandibles and two sets of palps. The mandibles can dominate the whole head, as they do in the male stag beetle.

In the diagram opposite only two head areas are shown, the epicranium and the labrum. If we had to be more precise the subdivision would be taken further, but the recognition of the head parts is so difficult that for our purposes any further breakdown would confuse rather than clarify. The Goliath beetle is an example: he is the handsome fellow on the dust jacket of this book; an entomologist could doubtless recognise the sub-divisions of the head, and even indicate the difference between the functional and the ornamental. I certainly couldn't.

The head parts of some insects, like the wasp or the grasshopper, are quite easy to distinguish once one knows what to look for. The disposition of parts in our diagram is very closely approximated in the studies of a hornet's head on the two following pages, but no single diagram can possibly cover the innumerable forms that the head of an insect may assume.

We are concerned with what we can see. What we can see we may be able to identify from the diagram. We draw it anyway.

This diagram is more helpful as a guide to nomenclature of parts present and visible than as an aid to drawing. You will find that rarely does the particular insect in hand stick clearly to the rules.

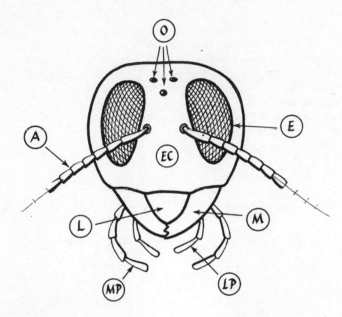

EC	Epicranium.	L	Labrum.
O	Ocelli.	M	Mandibles.
E	Compound eyes.	MP	Maxillary palps.
A	Antennæ.	LP	Labial palps.

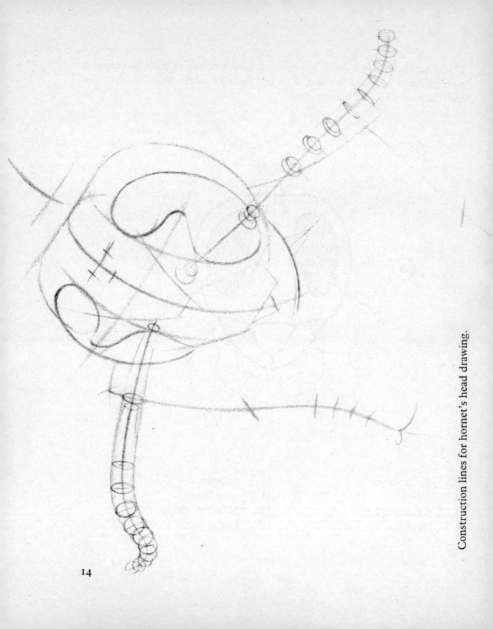

Construction lines for hornet's head drawing.

14

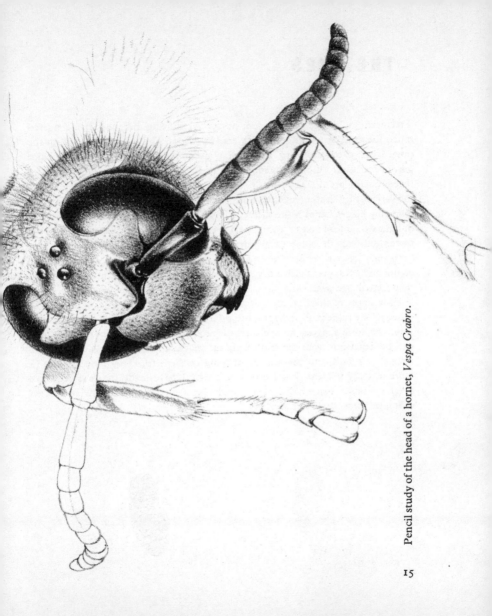

Pencil study of the head of a hornet, *Vespa Crabro*.

THE EYES

THE ocelli, or simple eyes, present no special drawing difficulty, being treated much the same as any other glossy convex object. The compound eyes on the other hand, need great care. In the dragon-fly opposite, they occupy the major part of the head, and must be modelled up skilfully in order to retain the translucent quality peculiar to them. Observe where the highlights occur; they are not the surface highlights of an opaque object, but the cumulative effect of many tiny reflecting planes beneath the surface. They happen moreover, where the source of light would lead you to least expect them. I have tried to illustrate this in the sketch, although the subject really demands colour.

In some cases a certain degree of licence may be taken in the drawing of the compound eyes, particularly if your drawing is intended to be more decorative than factual (see page 58).

Four stages of this sort of treatment are also illustrated opposite. This technique in one respect, is perhaps more informative than a strictly correct drawing would be, for it suggests more clearly the multi-lensed character of the eyes. You will be departing from the truth only inasmuch as your lenses will be square instead of round, and you will be drawing one lens for every nine, twelve, or more actually present. For reasons of clarity I have made the four sequence diagrams much coarser than they should be; something nearer the two larger examples below should be aimed at.

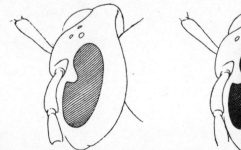

The huge compound eyes of the dragon-fly, *Libellula depressa*,
showing the large oval anterior ocellus;
two smaller ocelli are situated behind the bristle-like antennæ.

THE ANTENNAE

ON the facing page I have drawn some, but by no means all, of the different types of antennæ that you may encounter.

These extremely sensitive organs of scent and touch stem from the front of the head, near the compound eyes, They can vary enormously in form and in number of parts. They can be diminutive as in the dragon-fly, or longer than the entire insect as in the cockroach. Their articulated structure is often very much like our row of flower pots. The parts (or pots) will differ in number, shape, proportion and texture, quite considerable differences occurring in the same antenna.

The first segment, that attached to the head, is called the scape, the second segment is the pedicel, and the remainder are termed collectively the flagellum. The first two segments are usually quite different in shape from the rest of the antennæ, and sometimes quite a remarkable change occurs in the last few segments. When drawing antennæ comprising a countable number of sections, care should be taken to draw the correct number, as this is likely to be a constant. There are safe exceptions as with the setaceous antennæ of the cockroach, or the Giant Grasshopper, where, not only is the number of segments variable, but the size of drawing will probably only permit a tapering curve to be drawn. When in action the antennæ are normally carried in a forward position, but the longer types may be trailed back over the body when flying, see Acrocercops on page 63.

Studies of antennæ
Left: Stag beetle, *Leucanus cervus*
Below: Violet ground beetle, *Carabus violaceus*.

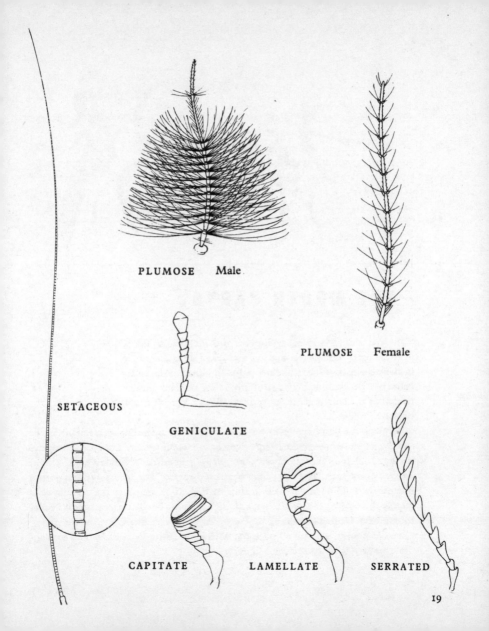

PLUMOSE   Male

PLUMOSE   Female

SETACEOUS

GENICULATE

CAPITATE   LAMELLATE   SERRATED

19

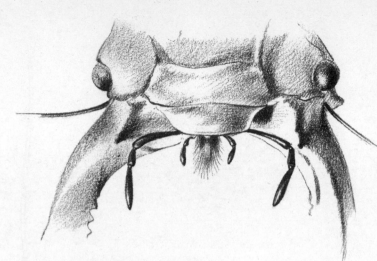

THE MOUTH PARTS

THE size of one's drawing seldom permits much to be made of these parts. Unless the angle of view is an unusual one, it is likely that part of the maxillary palps and most of the labial palps will be concealed. The structure of the palps is similar to that of the legs, and they operate much as a human finger does when flexed.

Whereas the palps are never very impressive, the mandibles can sometimes be the dominant feature of the head*, even of the whole insect. They are not always designed solely as feeding implements, being sometimes formidable weapons of offence or defence. The male Stag beetle appears to use his magnificent spread mainly for holding the female during mating. The shape of the mandibles is largely dictated by their function, although in some of the larger tropical beetles the function is often obscure.

*See *Odontotermes obesus* on page 64, where the entire head is devoted to mandible operation, to the exclusion of eyes.

Studies of two types of mandible

Above: Tiger beetle,
Cicindela campestris

Right: Violet ground beetle,
Carabus violaceus

THE THORAX

THIS is the central mass of our insect, which contains the mechanism of loco-
motion. A diagram of the subdivision will be found in any good book on entomology, but it won't help us a great deal in our drawing, for again the shapes of
parts can baffle the lay eye. I shall have to use some diagrams however, in order to
locate parts we may be dealing with later on.

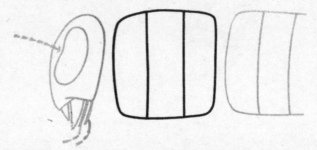

The first subdivision is into three, the prothorax, that nearest the head, the mesothorax, or middle portion, and the metathorax, the section attached to the abdomen.

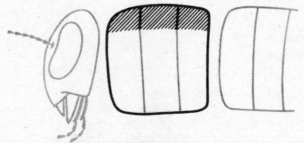

These three main divisions are divided further into an upper or dorsal region,
called the notum, each piece being given the same prefix as the three main sections, i.e. pronotum, mesonotum, and metanotum respectively.

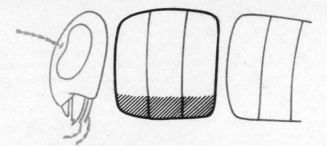

An under or ventral region, called the sternum, prefixed pro-, meso-, and meta-

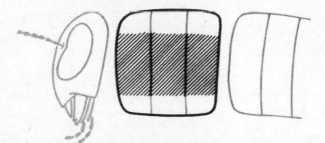

And an area in between called the pleuron, prefixed as the rest
Thus- pronotum + propleuron + prosternum = prothorax, and so on

The disposition of attachments is as follows:

The prothorax carries the head and the front legs, but never wings.

The mesothorax carries either the fore-wings in an insect possessing two pairs of wings, or the only wings in a two winged insect, or the elytra in a beetle, and the middle pair of legs.

The metathorax carries either the halteres, or the hind wings in a four winged insect, or the true wings of a beetle, the hind legs and the abdomen.

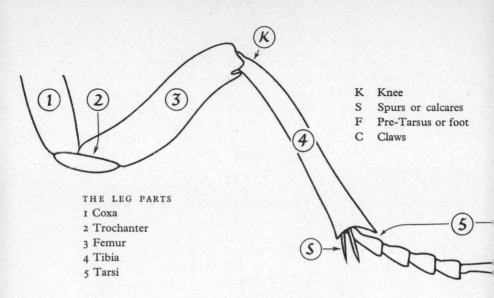

K   Knee
S   Spurs or calcares
F   Pre-Tarsus or foot
C   Claws

THE LEG PARTS
1 Coxa
2 Trochanter
3 Femur
4 Tibia
5 Tarsi

THE LEGS

THE most that can be said by way of a rule concerning the legs is that they are always six in number, and the number and names of parts is reasonably constant. Any departure from the latter will be most apparent at the foot end, where the tarsal segments may be less than the five shown in the diagram, and the claws may be furnished with different processes between and under them. The three pairs of legs stem from the ventral or underside of the three thoracic sections. When used for travelling they operate as a pair of alternating tripods, three legs supporting (fore and hind on one side with the middle of the other side), while the other three are moving. The legs are not only used for walking however, and the many ways in which different insects have modified their legs for other purposes have resulted in considerable variety of shape and proportion. The hind femur of the grasshopper has been enlarged in order to house the super-muscles it requires for jumping. With the predatory mantides the femur and tibia of the foreleg is equipped with interlocking spines, making a wickedly efficient trap for its victims. The need for burrowing tools has transformed the forelegs of the Mole cricket out of all recognition to the lay-eye, and in some aquatic insects the tarsi have become articulated oar-blades. The joints between leg-parts are variations of a basic ball-and-socket principle, sometimes flattened to a hinge of limited lateral movement, sometimes almost universal.

Drawing of inside rear left leg, showing calcares

Outside rear left leg

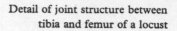

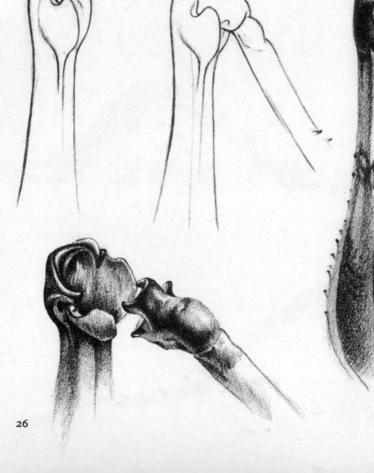

Two approaches to the drawing of wings
One relies chiefly upon highlight and shadow areas,
while the other depends almost entirely on vein structure

THE WINGS

THE wings of an insect are astonishing pieces of engineering, both in structure
and in function, the ratio of wing-area to body mass often confounding our laws
of aero-dynamics. Designed to operate at hundreds of beats per second, they
must be incredibly strong for their bulk. They are in fact, membraneous sacs,
giving the wing a double layer, like a flattened polythene bag, and strengthened
by means of ribs or veins. These veins, which are actually tubes, are not laid out
arbitrarily, but follow a well-planned arrangement, to suit the needs of the particular insect. Great care must be taken to draw them correctly, if your drawing is
to be taken seriously, for they are important features of classification. There can
be either four clearly separated wings as in the dragon-fly, or two pairs linked so
closely as to appear as one, as in the bee, or one pair only as in the true fly. They

may be invisible when not in use, as in the earwig, or almost non-existent as in the female cockroach. In some the forewings have developed into protective covers for the hind wings, called the elytra, which although having no propelling function, may well provide some degree of lift to the insect when in flight. Propulsion in this case being the job of the hind wings. In others, where the propulsion is left to the forewings, the hind wings have shrunk to tiny knobbed stalks, called the halteres, see opposite.

Although so reduced in size, these are vitally important organs of balance, and such an insect could not fly without them. The halteres are composed of three parts: a basal part called the scabellum, which is attached to the metathorax, a thin stalk called the pedicel, which terminates in a knob called the capitellum. If the halteres are visible in your specimen they must be drawn, although your drawing is unlikely to be large enough to show the three components. When not in use the wings are usually folded away in some fashion. An exception being the dragonfly who rests with them spreadeagled. They may be folded vertically over the back, or overlapping, flat along the back, angled over the back like a tent, or stowed away out of sight. Where the wing area necessary to flight is greater than the space available for stowing, ingenious systems have evolved. The locust family, for instance, can accommodate the length of wing but not the breadth, so the wing folds in an accordion or fan fashion, longitudinally. Others like the beetles have insufficient space under the elytra for either the length or breadth of extended wing, and a wonderful system of two-way folding has been developed, see page 55.

One of the most complicated systems occurs in the humble earwig, who really does get a quart of wing into a pint sized elytra. When drawing the veining of a wing you may not be able to see all of the system, some being obscured or confused by the overlapping of parts, folds, or bright highlights. In which case draw only the portions you are certain of, fading them off into areas of highlight or shadow. The highlights on a wing are usually crisp and well defined; draw these accurately and they will imply the correct position of veins that you cannot perhaps see. Above all, do not guess at vein structure, better far that some be lost to view than put in the wrong place. Highlights and shadows can be coaxed into more helpful places by moderate variation in your source of light, but don't make any drastic change of direction or contradictions will occur.

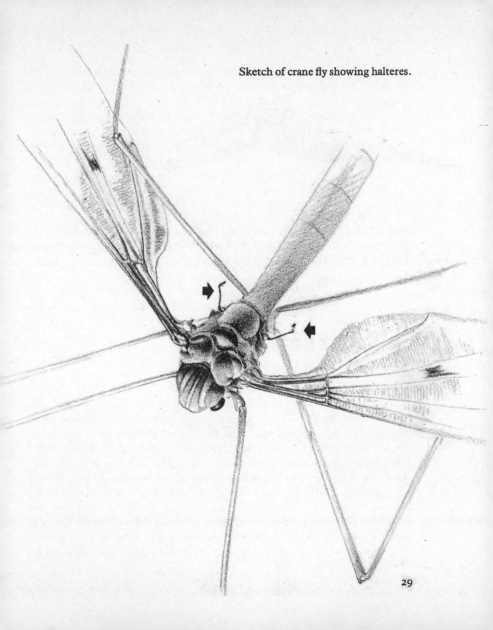

Sketch of crane fly showing halteres.

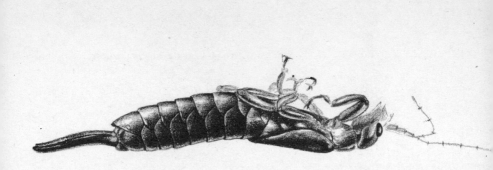

This drawing of the earwig, *Forficula auricularia,* shows the arrangement of the abdominal plates, and the kind of limb contortion that occurs in a chloroformed insect. The correction of this condition will be considered later on.

THE ABDOMEN

THIS third mass houses the organs of digestion and reproduction, and is the most flexible of the three. The plates, or sclerites, which may be eleven or less in number, are not as separate each from the other as they appear to be. Underneath is a continuous, pleated membranous sac, to which the dorsal and ventral plates are attached in ring formation, the rear edge of each overlapping the forward edge of its neighbour. Again very much like our row of flower pots, but this time half pots. The proportion of the plates, each to the other, is variable, the differences being most apparent at the ends of the group. The front segment may be so large as to embrace most of the abdominal mass, or joined to the thorax so neatly as to appear part of it. The most interesting part, from our point of view, is likely to be the last, or distal segment, where all manner of modifications are

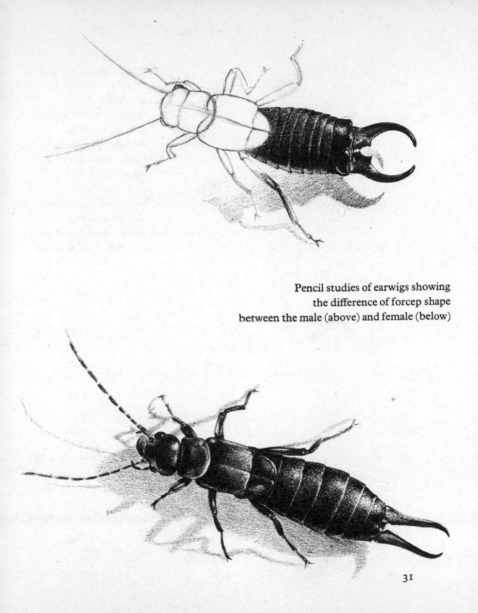

Pencil studies of earwigs showing
the difference of forcep shape
between the male (above) and female (below)

31

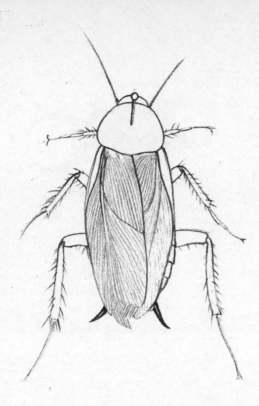

Rough sketch of
a cabinet mounted
specimen of the
common cockroach,
Blatta Orientalis,
showing the position
of the antenna-like cerci
This sketch
also illustrates the
deceptive suggestion
of abdominal legs,
when seen from above,
mentioned on page 10

possible, according to the needs of the species. It is here we find the antenna-like cerci of the cockroach, page 33, the businesslike ovipositor of the female grasshopper, page 61, the forceps of the earwig, page 31, and the sting of the wasp. Quite a difference of shape is often present between the sexes of the same insect.

Our list of component parts is now complete, but before we can start work, we must consider ways of obtaining and preparing specimens.

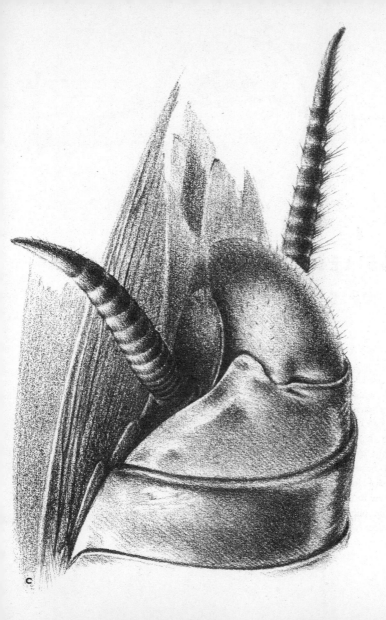

Close-up study of the cerci of a cockroach *Blatta orientalis*.

33

COLLECTION AND PREPARATION
OF SPECIMENS

By far the most interesting and the most satisfactory way of providing yourself with specimens for study is to catch and process them yourself. In this way, it is often possible to glean some information on their natural behaviour, feeding habits, wing position at rest etc, before actually capturing them. If this subject is altogether new to you, the mere thought of handling live insects to this extent may well discourage you: it did me for quite a while. In this case, almost any specimen you care to ask for may be bought, mounted and labelled, for astonishingly little cost. But more of this method later. Let us first deal with the live insect. Since I have to limit myself as far as possible to the drawing of insects, the procedure for hunting and catching I must leave to any of the excellent books now available to the amateur naturalist. We will assume then, that you have found a suitable specimen, made such field notes as were possible on the spot, and brought the insect home. It is a good idea to bring also some of the leaf-mould, moss, twigs etc, amongst which your specimen was busy when encountered. The next stage should be to house it in a container that permits undisturbed observation; a small aquarium with a cover is ideal for the larger insects, but really small creatures will be observable only in a relatively small container, such as a large test-tube. Some insects will even cooperate. The earwig, for example, is contact-responsive and seems to enjoy lying against things. If placed in a glass container, it will press itself into close contact with the glass side, and quite unhurried study of the live insect is thus possible. Since we shall require our insect to behave naturally whilst under observation, we must endeavour to furnish its temporary home as naturally as we can. A thin layer of soil, a few small stones, one reasonably large twig, and topped off with the odds and ends you brought back with him. Don't overdo the furniture though, or you will never see the lodger. Now the tank and its occupant should be left quite undisturbed, in a position sufficiently well-lit to allow easy study, but not in direct sunlight which would probably drive it into hiding. Your guest will probably devote all his energies immediately towards means of escape, and since no useful work can be done while he is panicky or disgruntled, a day or so must now elapse for 'calming down'. This waiting period may be profitably employed at the library in identifying the insect, and learning all you can of his habits. Find out what the natural food is and provide some, this may take his attention away from the battle with the glass walls, and give you an opportunity to study his feeding positions. If any of this information is unavailable at the library, a telephone call to the British Museum of Natural History rarely fails—the resident experts there are most helpful and friendly. After a time, when your insect has calmed down and is pottering about his new terrain, you can start some preliminary notes. A large stand lens can be used for this work, but nothing powerful will hold a moving insect in focus long enough for accuracy. These notes will perforce be sketchy, seldom complete, and only an aid to more accurate work later on. Concentrate at this stage on details of natural stance, positions of legs, flexibility of the tarsi, the curve and range of the antennæ, the operation of the mandibles and palps, anything in fact that is likely to be of assistance when ultimately mounting the dead specimen in a life-like pose. For dead it must be, if an accurate drawing is the aim; a live (and lively) insect is an impossible model—see title page. Your insect will not co-operate to the extent of dying in a suitable pose: it may be quite contorted, hence the need for these preliminary notes. Having made these sketches, the time comes for despatch. There are several methods for this. The professional entomologist usually favours the cyanide bottle, which I am told is quite safe, but with two experimentally-minded young daughters at large I personally will have nothing to do with it. Crushed laurel leaves under a perforated cover in an airtight tin is an old and reliable method. I use a pledget of cotton wool soaked in chloroform in a wide-necked fruit preserving jar. This method has one slight drawback in that the subject is somewhat contorted in the process, see page 30, but this is quite easily corrected later on. I have read that chloroform can stimulate some insects to the extent of damage, but I have had no cases of this myself. There is a killing fluid obtainable that I believe has no vices, but as yet I have not used it. I must cover myself at this point by admitting that the following procedure, which may well horrify any real entomologist, is my own method. I have found it simple and in every way satisfactory. I place my insect in a wide-necked fruit preserving jar, and hang a piece of cotton wool soaked in chloroform over the edge, gripped by the lid when closed. This is to keep it clear of any contact with the specimen. The time taken in killing varies with different insects, and appears to have nothing to do with size. I have found an ant much more resistant than a stag beetle. I usually allow an hour after all movement has ceased. If too much time is allowed

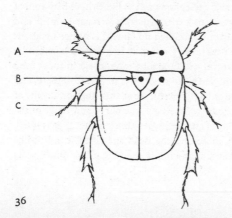

A

B

C

Place the fixing pin where it will not damage an important feature of the specimen.

Legs may be set to the desired angle by means of crossed pinning.

D shows how a joint may be held up or held down depending upon whether the pins cross over or under the leg.

E shows a leg being set with the tarsi making contact with the ground.

F shows a leg being set in the tiptoe stance preferred by some insects.

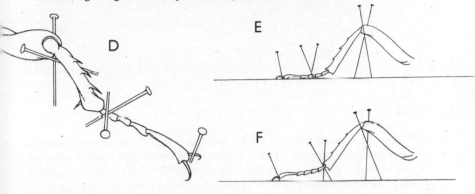

to elapse, the insect will have stiffened into its contorted position, and re-posing will be difficult. Your specimen may now be transfixed to its base-board by a central fixing-pin, the positioning of which will need some care. Whenever possible, I place it on one side of the thorax A. In this way, anything that it obscures or damages can still be found intact on the other side. Placed centrally, it can obliterate a feature of which there is but one. For this reason, I never transfix a beetle through the scutellum, B, the small shield which is part of the mesothorax, and is an important feature. A pin through this may wreck it entirely. You may pin through one of the elytra, C, if the proportion of your specimen makes this a more suitable place, but only if you are certain that you will never require to open the elytra and the wings; (if you feel at this point that the chief character in the drama is getting a somewhat raw deal, rest assured that his end has been infinitely more gentle than if left to nature). The following diagrammatic sketches show the order of pinning that I have found to be best.

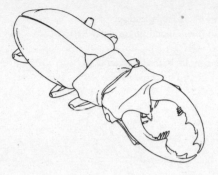

Beetle to be posed, showing the sort of hunched-up condition it may well be in at the outset.

For this operation you will need a pair of forceps, a mounted needle, and a supply of extra-fine pins, which are made in various lengths especially for this sort of work. Ordinary household pins may be used, but are not really suitable, they take up too much room, are clumsy to insert and displace too much of the

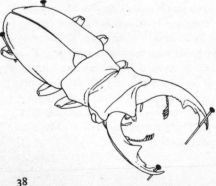

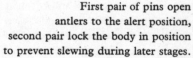

First pair of pins open antlers to the alert position, second pair lock the body in position to prevent slewing during later stages.

Next pairs strain the femoral
sections into position.
Heads of pins referred to in each
diagram are blacked in.

fixing-board. When pinning out a specimen, commence with the largest and
strongest joints, and work progressively through down to the last and most
delicate parts. I have chosen the male stag beetle for these diagrams because
his size makes for clarity and he has more than the average parts to be arranged.

Each leg will now need a pair of crossed
pins (only three pairs shown)
to control the position of the tibia,
and its angles with both the femur and tarsi.

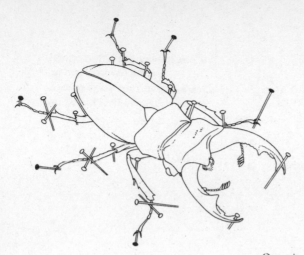

One pin per foot is usually enough
both to splay the claws
and to control the curve of the row of tarsi.

Lastly, one pair of pins to hold the antennæ open,
and as many pins as needed
to do the same for the palps.

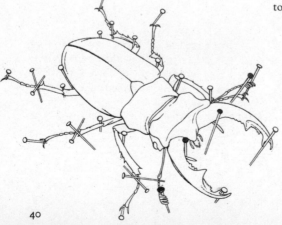

40

It is at this point in the proceedings that I find myself not nearly cold-blooded enough for comfort, and I replace my specimen, board, pins and all, into the killing jar, where I leave it overnight. It's a good idea now to give the specimen a day or so to set off completely. Before unpinning it entirely, release one limb only, and test it with a loosely held needle; if it feels rigid proceed with the remainder. Now pin your set insect, with its label, to a piece of $\frac{1}{4}$ inch balsa wood, large enough to cover all extremities. Despite the fact that normally handling is done by the pin, I have found that unless the need arises for removing the insect to study its under parts, risk of damage is lessened considerably if it is thereafter handled only by the board. Fixing is normally made into sheet cork, but much less force is needed when using balsa wood, an important consideration when fixing a delicate specimen so that its feet just make contact with the board. It is also possible sometimes to engage the points of the claws into the surface of the wood, making a perfect two point contact with the ground when set.

Don't make your fixing board too small. Allow generous margins for safe handling.

Bumble bee, *Bombus terrestris*, mounted as a cabinet specimen with its wings outspread.

BOUGHT SPECIMENS

N o w let us consider the insect you have bought from a naturalist, either because you prefer not to do your own killing, or because the insect you need is a foreigner and not obtainable in the live state. You will probably be supplied with a cabinet-mounted specimen, that is, one mounted in a spread-eagle fashion, in order to reveal the utmost information in one specimen. The arrangement of parts in this case will almost certainly be unnatural, and some adjustment will have to be made if your drawing is to appear life-like.

On no account attempt to alter the pose of such a specimen until you have relaxed it. This is an interesting task, but can only be really successful if your specimen is a perfect one. If it has at any time been repaired or if, as sometimes happens with larger insects, it is a composite insect, made up of parts of two or more specimens, it will fall apart during relaxing. It is possible to relax your specimen by leaving it for about 24 hours on damp blotting-paper in a closed container. This method I have found apt to germinate tiny mould growths later on, and now I always use a special relaxing fluid which contains some kind of fungicide or preserving fluid. This is very cheap: at the time of writing a 4oz bottle costs 9d, and is enough to process dozens of specimens. First fix your insect by its centre pin to a piece of $\frac{1}{4}$ or $\frac{3}{8}$ inch balsa wood, allowing generous margins for fixing pins and handling. Place the whole thing in an air-tight container (I use the same type of jar as for killing), with a piece of cotton wool or cleansing tissue soaked in the relaxing fluid. I think that 24 hours is far longer than is actually necessary, but the penalty for incomplete relaxation is damage to

After relaxing, the wings may be sprung back to the more natural position over the back. The bee is pinned to a base board between two strips of balsa wood, to which a bridge of thin card is pinned. The balsa wood strips must be of a thickness that will bring the card bridge into close contact with the upper surface of the abdomen. As the wings are carefully brought into position, they will try also to spring upwards away from the body. By placing two long pins at the angle shown here, the wings may be held back and down flat on the card bridge.

the specimen. To test the degree of relaxation, apply gentle pressure with the tips of your forceps to the lower end of a tibia. The hinge between tibia and femur should now move. If it does, the chances are that all the smaller parts will move also. If it doesn't, then further relaxing is needed. In obstinate cases, the fluid can safely be dropped on to the resisting part with a fine brush. When completely relaxed, the leg should articulate quite freely when manipulated with the forceps. Although the tarsi and claws should now be quite flexible, do not work them more than is necessary, they are still very delicate mechanisms. Resetting the legs, antennæ, palps etc is now comparatively simple, the pinning procedure being the same as that described earlier. The wings will call for some patience and a steady hand. Some insects carry the wings at right angles to the body when at rest, as does the dragon-fly; in this case, the wings of a cabinet specimen will need no adjusting. Other insects, like the bee and the wasp, carry their wings when at rest more parallel to the body. Both the bought specimen and the home-killed one will have the wings spread at right angles, the former because it is more informative that way, the latter because it died that way. If this type of subject is to be drawn as in life, the wings must be brought back along the body. This may be done by first relaxing, then careful manipulation with the forceps, pinning on to a sort of bridge (see page 43).

The most difficult resetting task, I think, is the raising of the elytra and the unfolding of the wings in a beetle, for which considerably more relaxing time must be given. The elytra may be raised very gradually by careful use of the forceps, but only in the right direction, outwards and upwards (see page 54) and may then be propped up for setting with two long pins. The wings can then be unfolded one at a time, and mounted as shown on page 56.

Another interesting job is the opening and fixing of the beautiful venetian-blind-like antennæ of the cockchafer. If you intend to draw your insect on a natural and irregular ground, set the legs and feet at the different levels and positions that it will later occupy. The stag beetle on page 59 for example, was mounted with the legs and feet embracing a wine-bottle cork, with a view to posing it on a branch of similar girth for the finished drawing. If you have both skill and patience, and your specimen is perfect, any position of which the insect was capable in life may be reconstructed.

Now to work.

Antenna of a cockchafer, closed and open.

Below: diagram showing method used in pinning out the antennæ of a cockchafer. The outside pins go in first, placed between the 6th and 7th leaves of the antennæ. These will control the angle between the antennæ and the head. The innermost pins go between leaves 1 and 2, and spring the whole system open. A little further dressing may be needed with a needle point in order to space out the leaves regularly. This operation is only possible after adequate relaxing.

DRAWING PROCEDURE

We come now to the point where our insect is posed to our liking, pinned to the stage, and the stage adjusted to the correct degree of angle and height. I have chosen a cockchafer for the following illustrations because in addition to a like-able teddy-bear appearance, it is of a good average size and possesses some interesting and adjustable features for drawing.

These sequence drawings are intended to show the procedure only, and not

Make your preliminary sketches, construction lines and measurements with the aid of the lowest powered lens, or any lens that will give complete coverage of the subject. This coverage should be generous, for a certain amount of distortion can occur near the lens edges. Try to see all that you possibly can with this first lens before changing to a more powerful one.

an exact picture of the results obtained with each of the lenses. Your first progress through the lenses will supply line information only, the process being repeated for the work of shading and modelling. Sometimes a final broad, overall rounding of the drawing will be needed, for which you will return to your large,

Your next lens will give you only portions of your subject. With this, you will be able to resolve secondary details such as joint structure of legs, exact number of segments in antennæ, correct shape of eyes etc, but do not stray from your original boundaries, which should be regarded as fixed, and any further information drawn within them.

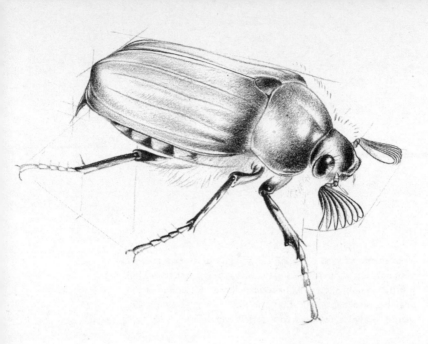

weak lens. When you are dealing with small features, such as spurs and bristles, or surface textures like rows of dimples or furrows, make certain that you draw the correct number, and in the right place, for they are often important items of identification, and not as haphazard as they sometimes appear to be. Go back to your large lens every now and then. You will find that you can see more than you did at first. The mind will translate earlier doubts in the light of information gained with the higher powered lenses. One other point worth mentioning is the importance of monocular vision. The difference between the viewing angle of the left eye and that of the right, which gives us our sense of third dimension and distance, is very considerable when compared to the size of the subject. Normally a boon, binocular vision is a hindrance to accuracy when plotting the relative

Your third and most powerful aid will give only small areas of your subject; with this you may, still keeping strictly within positions established by your weaker lenses, fill in any of the near-microscopic details that the size of the drawing demands—bristles, textures, foot details and the like.

dimensions and positions of our very small subject. Our drawing is going to be two-dimensional, that is either as the left eye saw it or as the right eye saw it. With a subject so near and so minute as our small beetle for example, the right eye may be seeing a straight profile, while the left eye may be getting an almost three-quarter front view. A drawing which attempts to include all the information available to both eyes can look very odd indeed. It will probably look bent.

Furthermore, it is desirable that the subject be viewed always through the centre of the lens, a condition only possible for one eye at a time. Therefore, all initial construction lines, measurements and relative positions of parts etc should be made with one eye closed. This is likely to be when you are using your first big lens, and since this is probably the only one where you could see the subject with both eyes at once, the smaller lenses catering for only one eye anyway, it usually means that all information is gathered with one eye, and only for the actual drawing do you make use of both.

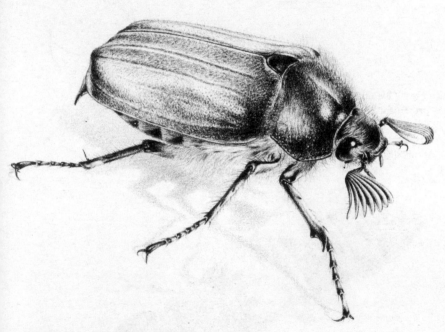

Cockchafer, *Melolontha melolontha*
In the interests of clarity, the three examples on pages 47, 49 and here show a greater difference between the information available to the three lenses than is actually the case.

This unfinished study of a rove beetle
presents a more correct picture of the development
through the first two lenses,
although the tones are darker than they should be.
At this stage the tones should be no darker than those of the unfinished
sketch of a grasshopper on page 61.

Examples of the sort of detail yet to be drawn into
the unfinished rove beetle drawing,
with the aid of the strongest lens.

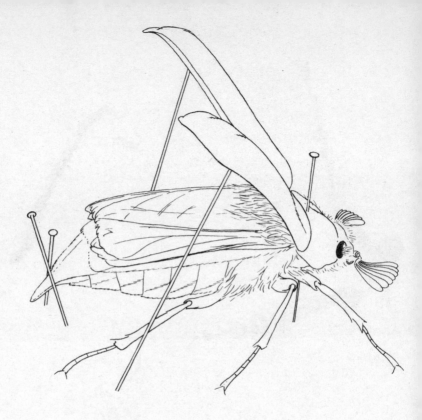

To return to our cockchafer: a further spell of relaxing, and careful use of the forceps will permit the raising of the elytra. First place crossed pins over the tip of the abdomen to prevent the specimen slewing round on its centre pin, then prop up the elytra to the desired angle with two long pins. When set, a drawing may be made of the beautifully folded wings.

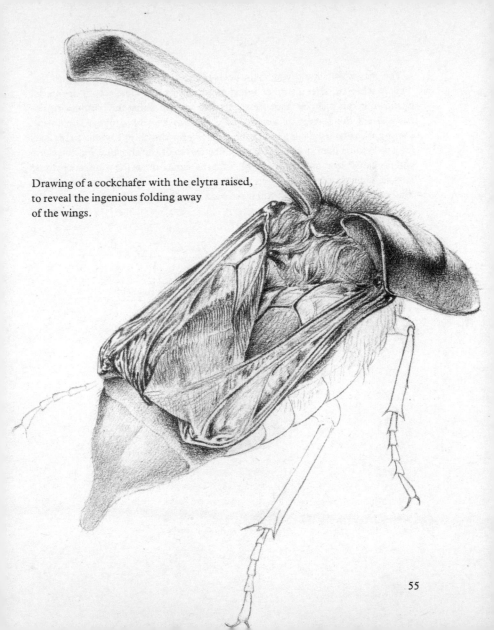

Drawing of a cockchafer with the elytra raised,
to reveal the ingenious folding away
of the wings.

You may now, should you wish, open the wings to their extended position. This is achieved, after a further relaxing, by means of a balsa wood 'dry-dock', as shown in this diagram. Care must be taken to ensure that the bottom strips of balsa are of the correct thickness, lest the wings be kinked out of alignment. During these later relaxing operations, parts previously set to your liking may tend to resume their original positions; the leaves of the antennæ and the elytra will probably close, and have to be re-set at the same time as the wings are spread. It is sometimes possible to soften parts by means of local application of relaxing fluid with a soft brush, which will leave parts already set unaffected.

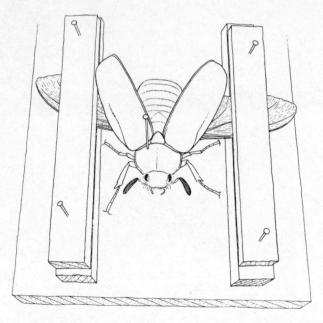

When completely set, a drawing of a cockchafer taking flight is possible.

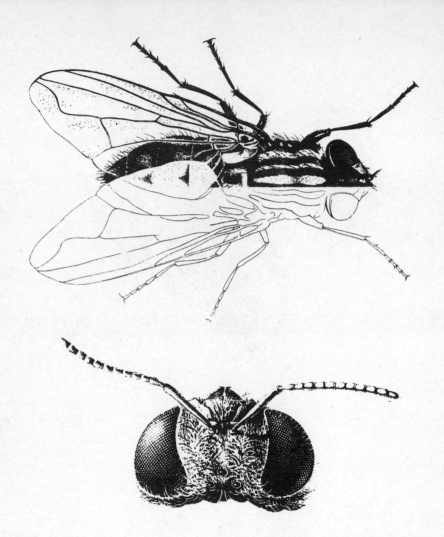

Examples of the sort of technique that permits the use of a formalised treatment of the compound eye, described on page 16.

Male stag beetle, *Leucanus cervus*, preparing for flight

Water-colour drawing of the weevil, *Cosmopolites sordidus*. The compound eyes, although not particularly small, are so streamlined into the shape of the head as to be almost invisible.

This preliminary study of the female Great Green grasshopper, *Locusta viridissima*, shows the amount of drawing possible with the naked eye and one large simple lens, when the insect is a large one. The tone is kept fairly light at this stage in order that further information may be added with the aid of a stronger lens.

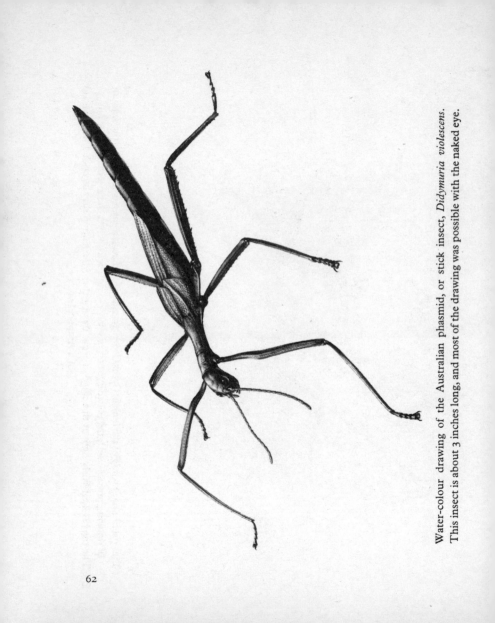

Water-colour drawing of the Australian phasmid, or stick insect, *Didymuria violescens*. This insect is about 3 inches long, and most of the drawing was possible with the naked eye.

Water-colour drawing of *Acrocercops cramerella*.
Another subject that had to be drawn through a
microscope, for although the wing span is only about
that of a small gnat, the colouring and scale pattern of
the wings are important classification features, and must
be drawn accurately.

Water-colour drawing of a soldier of the termite, *Odontotermes obsesus*.

This is not the sort of subject one would draw from choice; it is a soft-bodied insect, and must be preserved in alcohol. This, and the fact that it is something less than ⅛ inch in length, makes it a very difficult model. Anything as small as this cannot be drawn accurately without the aid of a microscope.